The Frequency of God

Mark William Jackson

The Frequency of God
Copyright Mark William Jackson ©2017

Cover Image: Silvia Schivella
Cover Design: Vivid Covers
Layout & Typset: Close-Up Books

All rights reserved. No part of this book may be reproduced in any form by any electronic or mechanical means including photocopying, recording, or information storage and retrieval without permission in writing from the authors.

ISBN-978-0-9876232-5-6

Published by Close-Up Books
Melbourne, Australia

For Silvia, Julia & Sonia

For England

Contents

The Frequency of God	6
Beat(en) & Saintly	7
The Sound of an Actual Man	9
fast food	10
Make Love, Not Warhol	11
vino e panini con Michelangelo	13
When I Last Spoke to Cocteau	14
Man Alive, Number 5	15
evolution of a Kind	17
Homeless	18
Life by Remote Control	19
what is real	20
Anti-Social Network	22
pill popping	23
Crackles to Life	24
Dirty Dancing	26
ode to disorder	28
No Tears Shed	29
From a Box of Old	30
To Your 18th Birthday	31
Hexagonal Variations on a Circular Thought	32
I Introduction	
II The Consideration	
III The Journey	
IV The Revelation	
V The Resolution	
Unspoken Love	36
& Art Floats Away Like Love	38
Meet Me in Paris	39

She Thinks (in Innocence)	40
to the star anise in my chai	41
This is Not for Valentine's	42
Crack	44
distance travelled over time taken	45

The Frequency of God

At a trash 'n' treasure market,
in an average town,
an old radio
encased in bakelite.

Plugged in &
waiting for the valves to warm
I took to the dial with a frothing sense of urgency,
twisting past horse races & rock & roll,
past right wing commentary,
        searching for the frequency of God,
long lost in digital audio,
        sure to be found
in the silver soldered
magic of a romanticised time.

        & there
at the end
of the amplitude modulated band,
        megahertz away from any generic noise,
    a perfect silence.

Beat(en) & Saintly

it was wednesday
& the wagtail blues
& bebop doos
fell like porcelain
from an angel's wings

hipster crooners
who clung to rags
like oxygen needles
danced on glass feet
stomping at the gin bar
& smoking leaves
of fortitude stripped
from a sandbox of lies

we waited for a taxi
while the moon bled jazz
over the new york sidewalk
insects laughed
at the show
mingling with saxophones
of stone
& now?

do you do do the new move
cloaked in ageless slipstreams
in the rat tat of hep cat culture
does your coffee pour whiskey
into your mind's cool blue fixtures

when your pen punctures pages
& when will you rest?
& is this a test?

historic light unsheathed
like a blade
to cut your arms
spill the blood
of fathers
like your blood
will be spilled by your sons
& what of your sons
do they float in spoons
in precious powder
crushed from the dragon's bone
the flame licks the steel
orange blue lights appeal
flick flickering images
in rolled eyes of
tangelo tint

when the spike pushes in
what does it take out?

The Sound of an Actual Man

The devil is in the detail,
in the teeth of violent dreams,
revealed in photospasms of the past,
of departures laden with lazy promise.

Do you remember strawberry fields?
Lines like lies crossing tees
 & dotting eyes,
lost in a visceral ineptitude,
sending sonar pulses through
a darkened history.

We are the soldiers in Sgt. Pepper's band,
cursing the silence in between the songs,
dancing in a frantic haze &
 boom boom ricochet,
paying prayer for a
slow motion replay.

fast food

the migraine visions
ludovican imagery
rapid fire persuasion
commercials selling a
united state
the great amerigan dream
fast food
the right to bear
arms with hollywood tattoos
sponsored by life in a can
be all that you can
rape land without reservation
only history changes
oh say can you see
by the dawn's neon light
one small step for man
one big mac for mankind

Make Love, Not Warhol

time-subject-film-light
Inspired by Ric Burns' Andy Warhol: A
Documentary Film.

The phonies are taking over,
the Jesus t-shirts
& ketchup stains.

Do you want me to tell you
who Andy was?
A mirror holder?

You move to the edge
& declare it the centre.
But now we throw hammers
at our reflections,
shattering silver thoughts.

Now the centre has been
cemented & secured -
trapped in a kaleidoscope
of commercial migraines,
the neon swirling like
an acid breast milk shake.

I'd film you sleeping
but that is now just
life / work / everyday.

If we slow 24 to 16
frames per second and
take time to see like a child?

Do you remember when
movies used to amaze?
time – subject – film – light

vino e panini con Michelangelo

I
sometimes it's necessary to mess with (reality)
our obsession with logic compels us
to mow our lawns every Sunday -
we'd all paint the grass if we could

II
blow-up!
blow your mind up
make your mind up
blow your makeup

III
wine & sandwiches in Rome
London owes you a decade
God's hand will rest on your shoulder
along the Po di Volano, at rest in Ferrara

When I Last Spoke to Cocteau
for Giampaolo De Santi

When I last spoke to Cocteau
he told me about a spin-
-ning game he played
as a child,
        I laughed but Cocteau
just smiled -   then serious
he said "I wrote to Satie
the other day but I don't expect a reply."
I told him I'd been to Arcueil
just after Satie died,
found a pile of unopened letters
near where he worked.

Cocteau didn't want to talk
anymore & said we should
go for a drink
he pointed to the end of the street
where a piano played the sound of clouds

        but I was too tired.

Man Alive, Number 5

Another dream of "normal" life,
the morning takes a knife &
plunges it into a weakened soul,
waits until time sears the pain & then
wraps it in a plastic bag of pregnant desires.

The bingo caller's lost his voice,
numbers fall to the floor, & are
left to roll around while the players panic,
clutching cards to their chests,
under house/cardiac arrest.

Sleep & the day becomes another,
dread falls like a midnight phone call –
did you remember to leave an
out of body message now you're a
thousand sighs from home?

But
    maybe you *should* call home,
to save *some* embarrassment of absence,
find out if someone's fed the elephant in the room,
and watered down the dandelion wine,
        (be responsible, man). No,

instead you eat a cancer sandwich
& sit on the side of the road
while cars race past
and a voice in your head screams
"BINGO!"

Evolution of a Kind

how do we rule?
        in words derived from Latin?
whispers from a dead tongue?

rolling with the punches
crippled by the lunches
feasts of fat men
suffering in splendour
priding themselves
on their wheels
and dreaming their
machinery dreams
but still
        just desperate apes
                trying to escape

Homeless

I am a thing / not a thing
elevated to the status
of object / product
a float between what
you've seen / thought you saw
      / ignored

the error of our ways
is the tragedy of our days
how long until O becomes Q
until the realisation gains a tail
& the question of de-evolution
is reconsidered by apes
on a production line

look, squatted in a shopfront
under discoloured blankets
the disgrace of our lives
thrown from the line
I am a thing / not a thing

Life by Remote Control

Ensconced in the images.
Injections from the 50 inch
frame across the room.

Bourgeois buttocks comfortable
on a lounge cut from old growth
forest by third world underaged.

Watch the news for sports updates,
interspersed with messages of the
latest products, requirements for a
new and improved reduced-fat life.
Abject images of war and hunger are flicked

to another channel where humans like
cattle file into a room to sing, their
country's got talent for schadenfreude,
- reality TV is an oxy   moron.

what is real

in this binary world
the liminal is lost
        only space between
        nowhere
and   now here

what is real

is it
the pen that slashes
across the page
in thrusts and swoops
like a swashbuckling hero
defending an honour

or
the dollar
wrestled from the grip of time
        a reward for trading
hours   away
calculated rates of
interest and exchange

the needle that digs in
        through skin
to deliver its
chemical images
what if the doors of perception
were cleansed

        and the reality
              drove us mad

or is it
the flickering visions of the past
captured on the mind's celluloid
or discarded on the cutting room floor
for not being
        of production quality

what is real
        real is the memory of things to come
        real is that love
that did not start
and will not finish
but just is.

Anti-Social Network

The new
Oxford-American
dictionary
has announced
its word
of the year is
'unfriend'.
'Love' has long been forgotten,
'Touch' is now irrelevant,
'Smile', 'Hope', 'Peace', 'Praise',
rendered to dusty print books
locked in open shelves
for all and none to see.
LMAO txt speak has won.
I am justified in my existence,
I facebook, therefore I am,
twitter ergo sum.
We have created our own Big Brother,
submitted to the cookie monster,
our lives are now just in-app purchases,
we've split our own personalities,
online identities.
Post.

pill popping

the dr. prescribes the latest pills
 - one in the morning
 - one at night
good for the heart
      age deflates
the balloon of youth
& immortality

I used to take my pills
from bathroom doctors,
prescriptions for
psychedelic meditation,
but now the doc says –
you've mapped the road
of excess, now
I pronounce you
heaven & hell,
you may kiss the ride,
the white rabbit done died.

now the CT map says *you are here...*
blood thinners & α-blockers,
taken with a glass of water
      & a grain of salt.

Crackles to Life

Under years of dust, at the back of the garage,
next to the old wardrobe that now holds
garden tools,
on top of cardboard boxes packed full of
things that are
no longer useful but too good to throw away,
rests the old record player.

I pull it from the mess of bits of bicycles & old
picnic baskets,
peel a record from its musty sleeve
& it crackles back to life sending out forgotten
analogue signals,
cutting through time at 33 RPM.

Now I'm talking 'bout my generation'[1],
Carnabetian[2] dreams & satanic sympathies.
Poet punk psychedelic stereophonic shamen
carry me back to days of
innocence & ignorant abandon.
The songs have remained the same[3], but the years
have moved on,
the doors may not be cleansed but the possibilities
are still infinite.

So the scientifically precise mp3 player bloated
with all its bits of data
can wait until I'm back in my car driving to work.
For now, I sit in the back of the garage,

in the chair we had in the living room before
the one we have now,
I sneak a cigarette so the kids don't catch me,
drop the needle, spin the black circle[4]
& float back to a life that has been stored,
no longer useful but too good to throw away.

---

1. Towshend, Peter. I'm talking 'bout my generation. "My Generation". *My Generation*. Record. Brunswick 05944. 1965.
2. Davies, Ray. Carnabetian. "Dedicated Follower of Fashion". *Single*. Record. Pye 7N 17064. 1966.
3. Page, Jimmy & Plant, Robert. The songs have remained the same. "The Song Remains the Same". *Houses of the Holy*. Record. Atlantic. 1973.
4. Vedder, Eddie. Spin the black circle. "Spin the Black Circle", *Vitalogy*, Record, CD, Epic, 1994.

Dirty Dancing

They've made a stage production
of a movie that was insanely popular
when you were growing up;
the trends of your youth now
have a retro curiosity to them,
like some sort of museum oddity.

Your music is now called classic rock &
your favourite albums are referred to as seminal
&
when a young band covers one of your old songs
&
you sing along your kids look at you strangely &
wonder how someone as *uncool* as you
could know something that they think is theirs.

Records have moved through CD to mp3
but a vinyl collection is to be held in awe
& video became DVD, & now blue, Ray
but the movies are just remakes.

Nintendos are now called Wiis,
Mario has risen bigger than Jesus,
& Apple is *the* product of choice
for the middle class edgy set
pretending to be artsy.

Now your rock stars are suffering from
old people ailments or reforming

for reunion retirement fund tours.
Bowie & Cohen, Prince & George Michael
all rang out their final chords.

Your favourite hangouts
have now been taken over by
cliché hipster cafés
selling pretentious single origin drinks
but you can't smoke or joke about
how contrived their record collection is.

One day they might
make a stage production of your life –
a black comedy
written by John Hughes.

ode to disorder

somewhere in the chaos are
the spontaneous mistakes
that make a day particular

paths that lie unplanned hidden
in erratic overgrowth

in the mess of photos
scattered throughout cardboard boxes
childhoods hide in fading tones

in the disarray of LP records
leaning across hi-fi shelves
hum the scratched songs of your forgotten youth

in the creaking cases of second hand book stores
great words wait to carry you

held in disorder lies a sweet bohemian breath
waiting to plant a kiss on your unsuspecting
cheek

eject your iPod and listen to the street

No Tears Shed

At the end of a life spent in utter pride
what questions linger in the dormant mind,
what life of chosen solitude led,
that would end in silence with no tears shed.

In ageing years when support is sought
from those whose love in frail arms caught,
what sorrow is absent from deathly bed
when a life could pass with no tears shed.

In distant home, in sufferance lied,
among strangers a woman gave up and died,
what hope of remorse when all prayers said,
when a family remains fractured, the mother is dead,
and a life passes in silence with no tears shed.

But though these stanzas have you crucified
it would be false to say that I never cried,
I hold onto tears for what I never had,
as your life passes by me one tear I shed.

From a Box of Old

From a box of old photos
fell the picture -
I am pressed against
my Dad's back,
cheek firmly between
his shoulder blades,
arms wrapped around
his belly.

We sit on a rock
overlooking the North Atlantic,
wind running through our hair
and I don't want to let go.
We stare through the camera
and I am happy,
a smile as wide as the picture itself.

From behind I can not see my Dad's face
but thirty years later
he looks worried;
something is about to happen,
the picture is about to be lost
amongst so many other
painful images, &
that holiday now
is so far away.

To Your 18th Birthday

They destroyed all that you had,
& left you in the dark space that was left,
to whisper of madness.

You wrapped yourself in sheets of cellophane
that fell to the ground with each painful sound,
every time someone spoke your father's name.

So you wrote poetry in a desperate metre,
drew faces of horror with blackened fingers
in the glass of a cruel mirror.

But the mirror was wiped clean,
and the poetry was put aside, classified
as the phase of a troubled teen.

And so to your 18th birthday when
you were supposed to do away with childish things.
You placed a candle in the fireplace

to warm your ashen face,
but never accepted that there was a place
for everything,
& everything in its place.

Hexagonal Variations on a Circular Thought

I never was what I used to be

I Introduction

I woke from a sweet sleep to find an old man
waiting in my reflection,
checking his watch & making calculations
in his ledger.
But I could only laugh as the hours washed
the days away,
& I turned off the light rather
than write to my father,
or stare further into the reflection of what is
or what might be.

I know I have to go back to where
the child is held,
prepare to fight, or worse,
confront the ordinary.
What if my whispers give no screams?
What if my screams give way to silence?
Then, what am I now?

II The Consideration

This now hasn't happened, yet
the memories are fading.

Consider the fluidity,
the ebb & flow of
time/memories, interwoven,
if you pull at one the other falls &
though the linear concept of time carries no
weight in my mind,
the persistence of memory burns its images
into a history
that's left wanting to conform with a calendar &
forced to comply with the old man's
calculations.

III The Journey

Return to your childhood home,
it's not as big,
the father's not as strong,
but frail, nearing his/our end, &
the happy times, the innocence
will hit you, &
the worries that held you then
will let you go
but will always...

Like when you look through old photos
& get a rush of sensations that
we are not here but there, &
whatever happened was fictional
but time folds;
age has acted upon us, catalysed, &
you are the product of what was/is,
& however the moments felt
they are now ingrained
into the most repressed depths of your soul, &
form part of the hole.
But what if the moments were manufactured,

just strategies, collateral damage divorced
from fact?
The feelings, though only manipulation
of false recall
still create the mind of a man, the old man,
still manifest the (reality) of a (life).

IV The Revelation

You were young,
childish & crazy.
You leapt at life
with abandon
like a drunken god.

But now? Responsibly
you pay your bills,
sort your garbage
& watch your diet.
Still hungover
from the trials of youth,
but now gracious &
somewhat subdued.

That's not to say you
fell into the machine,
but rather you consider your self,
you catch your reflection sometimes &
realise that the years have not taken,
that this then/now was/is happening,
youth may rest in the shade
but light shines on the vicissitudes of age.
You realise that you *are* the old man,
& it's only *you* who's calculating the time.

V The Resolution

Life is just a mix of

> • perception,
> • interpretation, &
> • the creation of "truth".

Existence is only a term we use
while we're trying to give ourselves meaning.

Therefore, in the context of meaning,
the world is only a representation,
a creation of the mind,
a surreal image,
> *ce n'est pas une vie.*

In (reality), to summarise;
there was no mother's loss,
nor no father's grief,
just memories, as they remember them,
& now?

A child's mind was folded
under their guiding hands
until their stories made the man.

But no more, know more,
now I am
because now I know
I never was what I used to be.

Unspoken Love

It hangs in the air
        between gazing eyes,
within a mother when she rubs
        for her unborn child.

You can see it in photos
        of an anniversary,
in the fingered indentations
        of a well worn rosary.

It spills from flowers that are
        placed to mark a grave,
echoes in prayers,
        requests to be saved.

It flows within the tears
        of those left to grieve,
waiting for a final kiss
        to give some relief.

It's left within the smiles
        when thoughts are brought to mind,
a sweet embrace that lingers
        after earth bound time.

It's when I think of my wife and daughters
        while I'm aching through the day,
it's in the ride I take back home
        and when I forget to say

that love is everywhere
untouched and unbroken,
love is captured in these words,
no longer left unspoken.

& Art Floats Away Like Love

Casting a street light shadow,
he leans against a wall
in a street gone to sleep,
plucks a soft tune on an
old guitar, sings, and drinks
in the resonance of the night.
The notes are like echoes, ghosts, smoke in the air.

... *meanwhile, across town...*
Hunched over a cafe table,
on a serviette he sketches
the woman across the room.
In blue ink alone he catches
the gleam in her eye as she
dreams her own dreams.
He folds the picture under his cup just before
he leaves.

... *in another place...*
He watches the people,
imagines their lives, talks
for them, creates histories,
drafts & redrafts poems
for them in his mind, but
never speaks a word.
In silence, the poems fall as tears from his eyes.

    & art floats away
like love.

Meet Me in Paris

Meet me in Paris,
you wear a rose
and I'll whistle the Marseillaise,
I'll buy us drinks
and we'll talk about times.

Meet me in Paris,
we'll walk the cobblestones
and fight off restauranteurs
until we find our place
where we'll sit in soft focus
while pedestrians blur around us;
a trick with a slow shutter speed.

Meet me in Paris,
on the bridge where our love hangs padlocked,
meet me at the café
at the end of our lives
and we'll drink one last time
and then tango into the after.

She Thinks (in Innocence)

She thinks because the moon is blue
that stars must whiten in its hue,
She thinks because the view is clear
that traffic lights just disappear,
She thinks if she could find a way
today will always be today,
She thinks because I wrote above
that I am worthy of her love,
She thinks the night is when to play,
I think her dreams of come what may
will one day find a day to say
I think she is all she is and may
be all I know she is to stay.
        She thinks I don't see her but loves on anyway

to the star anise in my chai
for Silvia

           you stung my tongue
with your liquorice wishes.
              I let my head recline
      as your flavours
             infused my mind
       with aniseed kisses.

This is Not for Valentine's
for Silvia

You aren't everything to me;
you don't make
political promises,
you don't offer a
compound interest rate
or discount on
combined insurance.
I don't think you could
solve Fermat's last theorem.
You don't come in 57 varieties,
and you can't boost my
phone's signal strength.
        I just wanted to dispense with
        the lip deep clichés.

You aren't my whole smile
but you are the corner of my eyes
that wrinkle once my mouth has
curled as far as it can.

You aren't my whole cake
but you are the sweet crumbs
I collect by pressing my
finger to the plate.

The Frequency of God

You aren't my whole day,
but you are there when I sleep,
and you are there
when I wake.

You aren't my whole life,
but you are the reason
I am not merely
birth and end dates.

> You aren't everything I love,
> but you are the reason I know what love is.

Crack

even though
I have Joy Division
at top volume
I can still hear the ice
in my whiskey
crack

distance travelled over time taken
for the brother I once had

the shortest distance between two points
      is a straight line like linear time

*

emotions attack me in a flurry of memories
& I, meant to be the 'strong' one,
am left drowning, trying to save you (me)
trying to reach back to you, to slow the
moments
but all the time time moves forward

      now, that time has gone
      back there where we played our games
running down the street using
our fingers as guns
making 'peyew' noises to fire a bullet
feeling the kickback, dodging the ricochet
         now the safety is off, you have
      grown into something else &
I have to keep you, the dark creature, in my
cross hairs

now if I think about the you back then
I laugh & cry
      we were so innocent because
we believed we were so innocent

but no, we never had the milk-like innocence
that every child is owed, that is bestowed
at their birth
  no, that spectre of our genetics was
always looming
& we should have known we would have to pay
our mother's past due accounts

   *

there's a crash coming
   lightning has struck the horizon
& we're counting the seconds
to figure how far away it is

   & when the thunder comes
we'll wince & brace
for the aftershock

these are our lives now

Acknowledgments

The Frequency of God first published in *Windmills*, Fifth Edition, November 2010, subsequent publications in *Best Australian Poems 2011*, & *Notes for Translators 2012*.
Beat(en) & Saintly first published in *The Diamond & the Thief*, Black Rider Press, September 2010.
The Sound of an Actual Man first published in *Rabbit Poetry Journal*, Issue 4, May 2012.
fast food first published in *Velour*, October 2011.
pill popping first published in *Rabbit Poetry Journal*, Issue 4, May 2012.
Make Love, Not Warhol first published in *Rabbit Poetry Journal*, Issue 4, May 2012.
vino e panini con Michelangelo first published in *Tincture Journal*, Issue 14, June 2016
When I Last Spoke to Cocteau first published in *Writ. Poetry Review*, 5 January, 2015.
Man Alive, Number 5 first published in *Tincture Journal* #9, February 2015.
evolution of a Kind first published in *Verity La*, 12 June, 2012
Homeless first published in *Page Seventeen*, Issue 12, November 2015.
Life by Remote Control first published in *Popshot*, Issue 4, September 2010.
what is real first published in *The Bacopa Literary Review*, May 2011.
Anti-social Network first published in *Miscellaneous Voices #1: Australian Blog Writing*, Miscellaneous Press, April 2010.

Crackles to Life first published in *The Interpreter's House*, Issue 63, October, 2016.

Ode to Disorder first published in *Underground*, Issue 6, April 2011.

No Tears Shed first published in *Underground*, Issue 4, September 2010.

From a Box of Old first published in *Rabbit*, Issue 3, January 2012.

Unspoken Love first published in *Miscellaneous Voices #1: Australian Blog Writing*, Miscellaneous Press, April 2010.

& Art Floats Away Like Love first published in *ZineWest 2014*, October 2014.

Meet Me in Paris first published in *ZineWest 2013*, October 2013.

She Thinks (in Innocence) first published in *PASH Capsule*, 4 March, 2014.

to the star anise in my chai first published in *PASH capsule*, 28 May, 2014.

This is Not for Valentine's first published in *Sacred Profane*, OWA Press, October, 2013.

Crack first published in *Make Your Mark*, Issue 7, March 2015

distance travelled over time taken first published in *Poetry & Place Anthology 2015*, Close-Up Books, April 2016.

www.ingramcontent.com/pod-product-compliance
Lightning Source LLC
Chambersburg PA
CBHW020703300426
44112CB00007B/503